LETTERS FROM A TATTERED SOUL

EASY LIFE LESSONS FROM A SOUL IN HER LATE TWENTIES

SHRUTHI SHIVASWAMY

This dedication would be incomplete if I do not begin with family, friends, teachers, work colleagues, acquaintances, authors, content creators and everyone who in some way contributed to my experiences and helped shape my views of the self and the world.

Having tried for more than ten years to start a book, I have never been able to as I always felt time wasn't ripe. But here, I dedicate my first book to the one human being who got me out of self-pity, helped me fix relationships and said "***Shruthi, Jee lo apni zindagi***" and also showed me how to do it.

Contents

Dad

Early To Motherhood

(Indian) Society

The Calendar Of Your Life

Butterfly Effect

Destined?

Sacrifice, Is It Worth It?

Darkness

Madness With An M.

Non-living Objects

The Root, Shoot And The Tree

Mom

Marriage

Within The Family

People Pleaser

Sister

Your Character's Name Is..

Brother

Peer Pressure

To Stay, Wait Or Leave?

God

Contents

Contents

Contents

Foreword

Guidance, good relationships, motivation and a positive environment, are some of the things that help one pursue their dreams. But finding strength to follow dreams when stuck in a storm of tribulations demands a resilient soul!

Shru, as I call her, is one such individual. I have known her for over a decade now and I see her as another example to reaffirm that *no journey is easy and yet no journey is difficult enough* to bury you permanently! This book would help you, the readers, to witness that not all fullpoints are an end to a story but can only be the begining of a new paragraph in the story of life, if we keep writing. When forced with ashes on top, strive to shake off the ashes and glow bright! Keep writing, just like Shru!

- **Franklin Christopher**, *Counsellor, Techie and Climate change ambassador.*

Preface

We are all born with a calling, sometimes we choose not to listen to it. Sometimes we try ignoring it completely but it keeps popping up wherever you turn. We try satisfying society's description of success but even after getting there, it feels like nobody really cares and you still feel empty inside. Life's lessons keep repeating until you get the passing grade. We often think that all this happens randomly and not consciously but once we start noticing a pattern, we understand nothing happens by pure chance, we come across things that we attracted a long time ago, that we obsessed over years ago perhaps.

They say we find destiny on the road we took to avoid it. I took one such road and buried my career and future at 21. Here I am 7 years later, towards the same goal I thought I had gotten rid of for good. My experiences are not pieces of advice, but my perception of them but they may make sense to you because they are not about rare and unimaginable things but very commonplace ones. In these pages you will find poetry starting with things personal and upclose like family, childhood and then escalate to darker things in life and then you will find them toning down to lighter notes like recovery, motivation and self love.

Hope you enjoy reading this book.

Gratitude

Forever grateful to *Zional Vijay* sir, who always made time to pray for me and my family.

My friend and yoga teacher *Indu Baburaj*, looks like you were sent to me for this very moment.

Thank you *Vrikshika Narayanan* for being the one listening 24x7.

Thank you *Srishty Agarwal*, my counsellor from *Sridhar Life School* who listened sincerely, helped me think objectively and understand my priorities. Special thanks to my nutritionist and trainer *Kaish Chahal* for considerately mentoring my diet and helping me maintain a great relationship with food, thanks to you I have gotten my kitchen straight.

Dad

Dad : "Why do you keep trying one thing or another? why can't you stop and just relax?

Why can't you just do what everyone else normally does?"

Me: "Dad, I really wish I knew why."

Early to motherhood

Me : Why baby did you choose me?

Unfit for motherhood,

Too old for excitement;

Too young to settle

Too naive to deal with everything else

That comes along with having a baby.

Too sensitive to deal with 'perfect' critics

Why baby, did you want to suffer?

Choosing this unfit mom who wanted many things

Baby: I wanted to see, how well you did,

When I come into your life;

And speed things up.

You didnt need to be perfect

But I knew you would love me

With more than what you can offer,

And I always know, your heart is always mine.

(Indian) society

Dare not live in your own bubble said the world,

That was very well living in its own

Often pushing, pulling and fighting when

They realised they were stepping on each others' toes

Those who shied away from the drama

Were often called "misfits".

I tried making bubbles like theirs and fitting in with

The ever popping crowd,

But it was heavy when I realised

That I needed to burst others' bubbles as well,

So I finally decided

I'd rather sit in the corner,

With other misfits who chose not to make noise.

The calendar of your life

We spend days that add up to years

Convincing people that we live upto their standards.

We spend a good deal of time

Trying to tell a compliment from sarcasm

And pondering over the subtle wounds that come

Often uninvited and leave a bad aftertaste.

Years go by and the fruit of gratification hasn't come

Then we spend a larger part of life,

Often tired and beaten than before

Realising that if we had just quenched the soul first,

If we had only just patiently worked true to our own selves

Void of expectating certain reactions from others,

Would everything have perfectly fallen into place

Much, much earlier.

But just this realisation- will free you, me, everyone.

"Just listen to yourself dude".

Butterfly Effect

They: Explain butterfly effect in simple terms to me

Me: If you believe little things can lead to big things often far, far
away

In ways you can never imagine, that belief is called the Butterfly
Effect.

Also me: But if you believe life is only a string of perfectly
controlled,

often dramatic and big things, then whatever the butterfly effect is,

It is of no use to you, my dear friend.

Destined?

How do you know if you are destined to do something? Or be
somewhere?

Try new things,

Take different paths

Be as impossibly far

But you see yourself getting back towards it

No matter what transpires differently

And if you are lucky (unlucky) enough

To believe that the universe is conscious

You will see yourself/ feel yourself doing it

Being there;

Even without knowing how or why or when.

But remember!

Whatever you are destined to do

Would never seem to weigh you down.

Or force you to be something

Drastically "unlike you".

In the serene lake where the soul likes to rest

You shall see yourself.

Sacrifice, is it worth it?

Any sacrifice is worth it

If you wanted it only to serve its purpose

And nothing oh so more;

Nothing more.

What we give,

What we throw about

Has a funny way of coming back

In ways we least expect.

If your sacrifice requires

Your kids to be indebted to you-

To the point they have to put themselves last;

Then perhaps don't make that sacrifice

And shackle them.

Or do the sacrifice and don't shackle them.

Any sacrifice is worth it

If you wanted it only to serve its purpose

And nothing oh so more;

Nothing more.

Darkness

No man victoriously overcame his own demons

Until ... he met darkness greater than his own.

In this premise, has the man (or the woman)

Two choices-

Defeat the dark cloud hanging over him

Even if that means destroying himself

Or become something very much like it.

Inorder to be able to continue to exist.

Never lose heart,

Asking "why me?" for-

You get nowhere in life

If you keep believing that you are perfectly incapable

Of any kind of evil.

The bigger the battle, the more glory in emerging victorious.

Madness with an M.

Everyone you know or don't know,

Is perfectly capable of being insane.

Atleast at some point of time in their lives.

For chaos and entropy

Always trump order and syntropy

In this measurable, visible universe.

It is no shame in being driven mad

Than the horror of driving someone insane

Purely for masking

The dark intentions lurking within.

And overriding and guilt and shame within.

Madness is okay

Intentional evil isn't.

Non-living objects

Things that don't live and breath

Can sustain life, protect the heart and

Feed the will to live;

Often doing better than what people can do

Promising reliability,

So much humility

Immeasurable serenity,

In all things that are

Non-living.

We don't often appreciate

Things that remind us of the good in life.

(P.S : Keep your laptop, your action figure, stuffed animal or your
headphones

as safe as they can be)

The root, shoot and the tree

I was always told

By everyone around me

From family, to relatives and astrologers

Directly or subtly

That I would amount to NOTHING, NOTHING.

I tried believing it but lo! Could I not.

Something about the prediction

Always felt wrong.

But I did somehow keep failing at big projects

I did always keep my faith in all the wrong places

And failures never stopped coming,

But I never, ever failed at giving what they call:

"One hundred percent"

Now I remember the Buddhist analogy,

For the tree, the deeper the roots in the lower world;

The bigger and larger the life is above the ground.

You can believe what you are told

But do ONCE listen to what you FEEL.

Mom

Mom , I wish I could take away your pain

From the past, present and future.

But not in the way you want me to

But this time,

In my way. For I tried once doing things your way,

And I am brimming at the biggest fall of my life.

I am not angry at you. I promise

Because you have only wanted the best for us,

But the world doesn't always mirror your goodness

I have exhausted half my youth

In trying to please you, in exactly your terms.

I have forgotten what makes me happy

I have forgotten what my pain threshold is

If I fail more and more again, I will end up dragging you all along.

Mom , I wish I could take away your pain

From the past, present and future.

But not in the way you want me to

But this time,

In my way

For nothing is your fault.

It is just the way it was meant to be.

Marriage

It takes TWO to tango my friend;

It takes TWO.

It takes two people to keep the ship afloat;

To drag it down smooth and perfect too!

It takes TWO to tango.

If you don't man the cabin

And give it to someone who isn't part of the seafaring

But likes to *play* captain;

You are going down my friend;

You are going down.

It is you two and you two alone

And if you don't keep up your end of the deal;

You go down my friend, down you go.

Within the family

Within the family;

Choose your battles wisely

If wiser, choose not to battle at all.

Even if you keep hearing

A war cry too often than necessary,

But that doesn't necessarily mean

You need to accept it as "the normal"

Normal things don't lead to abnormal events.

Just remember one thing;

In the face of provocation:

The man who has

People pleaser

If there is a sociopath who could care less

About any rules of society

(Whatever your social circle would mean)

And say there is a people pleaser

Who wants to be acceptable about

Every decision he makes

The society will most likely give them both,

The same baseline treatment;

The same kind of perks;

The same kind of safety

And the same kind of justice;

Infact the people pleaser can be

Branded behind his or her back.

Despite all the effort.

So you can be rebellious at every page turn?

No.

Be nice and genuine with as many as you can

But you don't you dare entertain

Everyone's priorities, everyone's pleasures.

So do not give away energy, like you would give away
compliments!

Sister

You have not been perfect to me

But you have always been genuine

And you have always kept me in line.

You have kept me level headed;

You have made me reinforce and believe:

Family is not a group of people

Who agree with you everywhere and in everything

For if that were the case,

It would cease to be family at all.

They just ought to be around

Even if they don't want to or are busy

You are fine just the way you are

Because you are not living someone else's image

Remember that.

And also sorry for taking all your Beyblades.

Your character's name is..

Be a blank slate, exist in the NOW.

Dare not believe the role the society gives you,

For nothing in life happens that fits

Into one person's narrative.

You may have a role to play

You might have to don unprecedented responsibilities

You could be a hero in one place

And a bystander in another;

In each different situation

In each different city,

Do not believe the narrative anyone, however important they are

Give you.

When you limit your thinking, you impair your judgment.

Observe. Learn. Respond.

Brother

You are not my blood

My dear brother

But you have done,

And been there for me

More than

What my imaginary brother could have done.

And mom and dad know that as well.

You have been a role model,

When I explain

See this is how boys can be like too,

They are not all the same.

You have always chosen

My well-being over what I want,

Just like any irritating brother would.

You have tried solving my problems

Like they were yours.

I hope I can someday, return the favor.

Family is not always,

Blood.

Peer pressure

Its not bad

Yes, peer pressure is not bad;

As long as you can leave it at school, college or the office.

And don't carry it often on the way back home,

And into the house.

Peer pressure is not dangerous,

As long as the neighbour's way of celebration

Remains of lesser importance

Than your own family's happiness

On that special day.

Peer pressure is not dangerous

As long as you don't get your daughter married

Because her cousins were married at a particular age.

Peer pressure is an assumption

Its not the reality of what people think of us.

People say things in public but think more about themselves than others.

It wouldn't hurt to remind ourselves of that now and then.

To stay, wait or leave?

If there is salvation in giving it time- stay.

If time is widening an already heartless gaping sinkhole- leave.

If people are getting hurt- leave.

If people need everyone else - stay.

If they will at some point sit down for negotiation- stay

If they still want their pound of flesh often -*literally*

and are unwilling to let go of the past-

That leaves you only one option.

Get help.

If it still doesn't work.

You know now what is left is all you will ever have.

If freedom is a bargain,

If you need to give a piece of your soul

To trade it off for other parts of your heart,

Then it was never a RIGHT but a COMMODITY

Now think... would you do the same to them?

Would you hold freedom hostage?

God

"If you are a believer" :

And if you are in pain,

And no human could help;

You turn to God,

He will most likely be listening,

Even if you don't say anything.

When you simply think:

"Please, help me"

It will be heard.

Help WILL be sent.

But inorder for you to be able to see it,

You must have believed

That help will MOST LIKELY come.

Dare I say, you are stuck in a forest;

And you see a rescue team flying by,

Until you make yourself visible,

They may not at all see you.

Similarly make yourself visible to a higher power

Whatever it might be. Again, only if you are a believer.

Prayer and faith

When we ask,

When we ask sincerely with no vengeance.

We are connecting with the positive power of creation.

The answer is never NO.

The answer might be "Do something different"

or "Get away from there"

or "You need to see something first"

or "You will survive this"

We don't see the answers

Because we only WANT one kind of answer,

Something that fits our liking and narrative.

But remember the answers are always there.

We can't make bargains with the creative power

Because what do we have that we can offer?

But we can always, always IMPLORE

Because the purpose of prayer is always to shed our "reality" and

CONNECT.

Politics

When all logic is fuzzy

When hate paints the town;

When all welfare is lost,

Humanity and art

They do enough, more than enough

They do exactly what politics should have done.

Elders

I am referring to elders who don't mean harm

In anyway to you.

Don't argue.

It doesn't work. I have tried it many, many times;

They only hear what they want to hear

They only ask what they want to know,

Never the whole thing.

Instead,

Show them.

We got this backwards

We strongly believe that situations must improve

Inorder for us to heal and improve ourselves as people.

But in reality, until we heal and improve ourselves,

We will not see a solution nor a way out.

Indeed, we got this backwards because

Everyone you turned to for advice said:

"Don't worry, everything will be alright".

Blame game

Blame game is an all powerful

Often repeated final strategy

To everyone protecting themselves but

Not the relationship- any relationship

It often overlooks;

Ignores the fact that

You cannot break something

That isn't already cracked.

And it would not have cracked;

With just one blow.

Family

As long as they are not intentionally toxic,

No matter if it costs an arm and a leg,

Your nest is your nest.

They may say things out of pain,

But family is family.

They will always have your back.

And even if you anger them,

You can always convince them.

Whatever they may personally believe,

Whatever they may hold against you,

Whatever flaws they may hold.

A part of them will always be rooting for you

Just remember that.

Escape from toxicity

Family? Extended family? School? Workplace?

Escape is not often dramatic;

Sometimes, escape is not even physical

It can be silent and subtle,

When you are removing yourself

A little by little, often one step at a time,

From the shut box that caused so much pain.

Escape from toxicity happens,

When you cut-off

From their reality.

When their version of you,

Is not your true version anymore

And you don't operate

On terms that are convenient to the abuser;

And you do not tell them outright,

Until you know, you are well past

The point of return.

Until then, it wouldn't hurt to give a chance

While you are silently protecting your mind

And heart.

Remember, excape from toxicity happens,

When you cut-off, from *their reality*.

Real hell

Hell and heaven are right here

But you can't see them just yet, they said.

And they probably were right.

The dimensions bleed into one another often I believe.

Humans are capable of inviting both into their homes.

For real hell is that in which:

Nobody but yourself know where you are

To the outside world, everything seems normal;

Sometimes so normal- it can often seem out of place.

Real hell is when you are made to follow

The *rules of heaven* to stay.

For you can escape that which abuses you;

But *not which chastises* you- that hell,

That is the real deal.

Toxic , so toxic you need an ER

Define toxicity?

Where should I begin?

With the types? degree ? and covert names under which toxicity
can exist?

The only true test of toxicity is:

You can FEEL it.

Even if it has been once,

Even if you have done it.

No matter how many alternate names,

No matter how many explanations.

No matter how much logic is attached to it;

If it is suffocating-it is suffocating.

Simple.

Real failure

Real failure is not being in a dark, deep pit.

Real failure is not realising you are in one

Real failure is missing out on all kind acts of salvation

Real failure is not having run away, while you could have

Real failure is losing everyone who could have made your life
better

Real failure is choosing one person at the expense of everyone else.

That, that is the darkest place one could be.

Because there really is no going back,

And definitely no decent, harmless way out.

Listen

Listen to those;

Who give boring but consistent information.

Do not be swept away

By theatrics, by dramatic claims.

Solid advice is like a foundation,

Its grey, regular, repetitive

And boring.

The devil is in "the denial"

The problem is not that the devil is evil,

But that she is smart.

She hides in plain sight

And impales me when nobody is looking

Makes me doubt my own red, bleeding, gaping wounds;

Heals me in public

And reopens the stitches when nobody is looking

Has an explanation for everything.

Has the perfect questions to

Shut my questions down

Knows how to push my buttons;

Hide in the crowd

And leave me screaming ;

She knows to set her minions on me

When I am just doing normal things

To make me look bad

For going about my day;

Chasing me with actions

Unthinkable;

Then accusing me of running away

Asks me to take what I want

But hides it when I need it the most.

Insults me in private

Chastises me in public

Because she knows very well

Women can't run from that which chastises

Clever, very clever.

The devil, is in "the denial"

Especially

When you can't see the details.

Tolerance

Be choosy about what you tolerate,

What you nurture consciously,

Grows;

What you allow to exist,

Also grows.

Much like a weed, an infestation or cancer.

That is just how things between people are too.

Please do not take this lightly.

- From experience.

Ignore

If you do not agree with a relative, friend

Ignore.

If you don't like tattle-talk.

Don't stay there, ignore.

If you don't like slander about someone else,

Ignore.

If explanation does not work,

Ignore.

If logic and basic values die

A slow death in the conversation,

Ignore.

Do not nod when you don't agree,

Just because you want to manage,

Just because everyone agrees. Just

Ignore.

Don't be like me,

IGNORE.

The fake laughter

He : Why are you laughing? Doesn't it hurt? Why do you have to
act?

She : People who act cry, they don't laugh.

He: Fake laughter, irritates me.

She: When misfortune comes in twos, threes and tens

You get so used to it,

Crying doesn't work anymore

You know, because crying never really helped.

Humour helps you survive,

Its also called dark humour I guess.

At a point you stop shedding tears;

You fall silent.

And when misfortune comes over and over again,

You laugh thinking about

How bad your luck must be.

It is not a fake laugh.

And who taught you, that grief means to shed tears?

Grow up my friend, grow up.

Good vibes, bad vibes

When you feel still,

You are not looking to judge

When you feel exactly in the middle

Exactly at zero

Not in the minus,

Not in the positive extreme;

At quiet, dim, stillness

Not wanting to be sure, not wanting to be master

Just with a clear, clear head,

An observer of the hills.

If you have a bad feeling

And it came out of nowhere.

If you have a good feeling

AND it lingers on and on..

The vibes are most likely true,

Also, thats how we catch up

With the long lost

Skill of Intuition.

Watch the Pattern.

The match made in heaven

The stars aligned -oh so perfect;

Even their heights matched-oh so cute!

Their families saw oh so perfectly eye to eye.

But their values did not,

Their priorities did not

Their aspirations did not.

Their dealing with crisis and differences did not

You cannot see or measure these things.....

What do you think happened after that?

Think again. Read this again.

Hate and tolerance

To avoid interactions with someone

Or to leave someone for good as well;

You don't necessarily have to hate them

Wholly, fully... upto the bone,

Why?

Because what if your tolerance to toxicity is

Already too high?

You wouldn't see the red flags

Would you?

Even if it doesn't hurt, like it hurt the first time

What is wrong by moral standard,

Is still wrong.

Speak up but softly.

Never tolerate something or be quiet about it,

Because you are tolerating someone

For someone else.

Relationships don't work with collateral.

Good friends, great friends.

Good friends help you out

When the favor is once.

Neat.

Great friends listen

To your rant, even if they can't help you out.

And they don't always agree;

They don't teach you shortcuts,

But just listen.

Don't ever, ever let them go

You will need them as much as you need family.

AND.... return the favor.

Over sharing

You can have a hundred friends;

But you need not over share.

You can love your friends just fine,

But you needn't have

Everyone's seal of APPROVAL.

You can always explain later.

Don't wait to get off the train track

Until the train is too close.

Skills don't wait, neither should I

One marketable skill.

Learn, upskill,

Start. Start today, start tomorrow

But start.

If fuelled by passion, all the better.

But having ONE of it,

Can make you feel richer

Than all of your family wealth combined.

No matter what they say around you,

No matter how many obstacles they throw

Down your path,

Fight through it all.

Trust me,

You won't regret it one tiny bit!

The one, the only

They always come

When you are not looking.

They turn your world

Upside down; More like the right side up.

They make you question what's happening

As if everything lead here to this very moment.

They reset your life

So you ask, God "Please tell me, Let me replay this one time in my
head

Before you tell me"

The dots connect now don't they?

Almost like art. And nothing was really said or done.

It feels all so much like homecoming

Often because

They feel the same way

And they are exactly like you.

But remember, they never come when you are looking..

Always look younger than you are

Get up, dress up, show up.

Even if it means

Your neighbour will be critical;

You will be taken less seriously.

Always try being

Active, young and enthusiastic

Than you are

Because what we repeatedly tell ourselves

What we repeatedly see ourselves as

Our body mirrors the same

Ten years down the line

The respect you got from

The aunty in the opposite house

Because you looked and behaved your age

Will matter less.

In health-

You are exactly what you think.

You are your first priority.

Exercise

Anything, just anything to get

Moving.

If days are dank and dark,

But if you can still move

Can still sweat

Can still focus on movement

Can still feel the air against your skin

You have won the war,

That day.

You can be like me,

Having no regular habit;

No proper time;

Have never had the need to;

But start.

If you could move that day,

You have conquered it all.

Money matters

You can invest,

You can spend;

You can even indulge or overspend

But try once making your own money

And try it all within your 20s

Experiment with your own earning,

When money is yours, you don't have to

Fret about upsetting people

With your purchase, investment

Or opinions. Ain't it?

People are a spectrum

Bad people, good people

Great people.

The worst kind.

Strong men, strong women,

Kids, not acting their age?

Young man giving advice for your 70s;

Older people with a child-like excitement

Weak people and unbelievable stories,

Whatever we have heard or seen,

How many years of experience you have had

There will always be the other extremes that are true.

NEVER generalise people.

NEVER.

People, are a spectrum.

People are a combination.

Delusional

Pride can be dangerous, yes

To the person carrying it

Oh so unknowingly in his heart.

But delusions can destroy families

And raze kingdoms to the ground.

What is more poisonous than delusion?

Is the sweet venom

Of SHARED DELUSION

Between two people who can't see

Beyond their walls of

Self-obsession.

Evil

When evil decides to sweep through

When it decides to act

When it decides to defend itself,

It carries no identity

Of caste, creed, language,

Distance, Race,

Religion,

Gender, age

Nor their relationship with you.

Evil knows no bounds.

Under-estimate

Never under-estimate

The power of meeting strangers,

The power of improving connections and

Sharing ideas,

In a good way or lesser.

They can change your life forever.

Never be stuck,

With the same set of ministers.

In reality- there are no strangers.

We are all connected, in some way or another.

It doesn't matter who you are,

How normal your life feels

Never over-estimate,

The security you feel,

Nor the time we have left.

Utilise whatever time you can utilise.

There will be absolutely no regrets later.

Self-respect

Matters not how many years you have seen,

Who they are to you,

If you refuse drawing a boundary

When you have lost self-respect;

What is left next

Will be your personal safety,

They will come for it

Soon. Very soon.

Image and connection

As long as nobody

Can connect with me,

And be convinced that I can be trusted

The image I have

Will mean nothing.

Genuinity always wins over perfection.

Also don't believe the perfect image of someone.

They will have a lot to hide.

Home

Nobody will remember how great

The meal tasted.

So always do the dishes.

People will always remember

Your cooking mistakes

Than the days you swept them off their feet.

People will always forget

How comfortable you made them

But will remember if things were messy,

Because of the same.

Until they see fever, bruise

Or blood,

They will believe you are sick.

At home, less is always more.

Even when you talk. Just keep in mind.

All this worst case scenario only. Just FYI.

Being Mommy

Even when they can't speak

They will always be trying to say something

Grandma can help,

Google can help.

Doctor can help

But only mommy can do it.

Only mommy can tell

When baby is full.

When baby is going to smile

When baby is going to throw up,

When baby is sick

When baby is cold,

When baby is about to be sick.

Only mommy can carry baby,

Like she and baby are one person.

The only real duty you have mommy is

Being choosy about the advice that is thrown at you.

And listening to your baby

And then following that advice.

Don't let emotions overtake you mommy

And don't let everyone dominate your baby's first year of life

Let it be his/hers and his/hers only.

Everyone and everything else can wait.

You can never prepare for the sleepless nights-

And the constant washing and waking

But you can get used to it

And before you know it, they will be all grown up.

Good, bad and vice-versa

Always remember

Your worst day

Can open doors to the best phase of your life

Your good days

Can keep you stuck

At your worst.

Something that was good for you

Something that was great for your cousins

May not be as good for you,

For destinies are connected

Not copied.

You never know

For the dots don't connect as we go.

But only when we turn to look

At how the dominos fell

To bring you here,

To this very moment.

Disease

Until you are sick

You would not know

How much time was lost

Waiting for what?

Disease puts your life

In a focus so pragmatic

You let go of wasting time

On things that never really had your heart.

Disease is the water,

That cleans up all the paint

And truly shows you

Who really is with you.

The eyes don't lie chico

Words can sound impactful,

Tears can roll down too

But the way people look at you

In hate or with love

Or where they choose to look

(When nobody is looking)

That dear heart, is the real deal.

The eyes,

They can never lie.

Disgust

What disgusts someone

Defines what they will

Never do.

What disgusts someone

Tells you what they will

Never tolerate.

Ask this in advance and

Confirm it.

Forgive

Give me a chance

To forgive

For leaving a void

Where once faith

In humanity lived.

Where once that faith

Tried so hard to overlook

The fault in our people

That we blamed on our stars.

Give me a reason

To forgive

Ill apologise too

Like I have done some great wrong.

I shall do that too.

Unlike you

Who denies it with more strength

Than it takes to

Just say sorry.

Unlike you

Who likes to throw people

Because they will come back

I stay until I know

I have been chipped to my bone

Give me a chance

To get things back to

How we all thought it was:

"Superficially perfect"

Most efficient way to revenge

Revenge is sweet, actually very sweet;

When you can take out

The bitterness of an experience totally

Revenge is sweet

Only when every action done

Is for yourself

And to get as far from the control drama as possible

Revenge is sweet

When you can tell them

"I couldn't have gotten so far,

So fast, without you"

Forgive your parents

If you know what made them do

Something you can't forget

But you want to.

You just know what did

You don't have to accept it.

You can just forgive.

Because unless you do

You aren't free from generational trauma.

And will be living in the shadows of

The bad years gone by.

Break free. Forgive.

Gossip kills self-respect

If you know the conversation

Hovers over boundaries that should not be touched

Whoever it might be about,

Don't indulge, feed or encourage the talk.

If you can, just leave.

It maybe your landlord,

It can be your neighbour,

An older relative;

It can even be your superior or teacher,

Don't ever entertain that.

Nothing screams ill-motivated, sad and miserable

Than gossip does.

Customize the swipe

What we feed,

Feeds us.

In the news feed,

Make sure you see posts and pages

Like, follow and subscribe-

Pages and channels

That align with goals

And feed your soul

More like a vision board

Or like flashcards carrying key points

Before a test.

Bend social media,

To serve your priorities.

Relive trauma- die twice

When you keep consciously replaying trauma

You reinforce your emotional reaction to it

The next time something similar happens.

Oh so wait- is it all psychology?

No, it also means

You would not react any other way

And you

Design your life

Because nobody else knows all the variables

Nobody else knows what works

And what works only partially

Never equate respect with

Absolute obedience.

Design your life

Based on how you want it to look

When you are older and retired.

Look to you and you only

Because ultimately you

Are your first audience

When you want it to be a certain way

You can't stop it from happening.

If manifestation didn't work,

Nobody would be doing it.

Languages

Learning a language,

Mastering a language

Can open your mind

To people unlike you

And open doors

To experiences

You never thought existed before

Also- It helps you battle

Any inferiority complex you may have left,

Because now you know,

You can move with anyone

And people are just like you.

Please, let the boys cry

Its only a shame

If your boy makes others cry.

Its not the new normal

And will take years

To accept that men can cry

But atleast while they are kids

Please let the boys cry.

Let them express pain

Let them calm down on their own

Conflict management

If it takes you;

Tears and crying to explain

You haven't done something

If they keep pressing their version

Of things, Oh so convincingly;

That is your cue

To stop explaining

And observe

If the blaming

Was deliberate

If they were waiting to do it.

You can never convince

Anyone who is convinced with

Their version of events. Period.

Journal, organise and tick

Every now and then,

Daily, if you may:

Write, achieve and tick off

Short term goals,

So the brain gets assured

The bigger and long-term ones

Are not that far away too.

Keep in touch with childhood

Drop a message to old friends,

Acquaintances and neighbours

Old people but fresher perspectives.

A refreshment

Gentle parenting

If the same results can be achieved

By normal talk

Than by force or rather by anger

Choose normal talk

With little ones.

When we condition them to respond

To anger and violence from us

We condition them to tolerate

The same in the outside world.

It doesn't have to be intentional

To cause irrepairable damage.

And it it took me 4 years of

Failed emotion control

To finally accept the same.

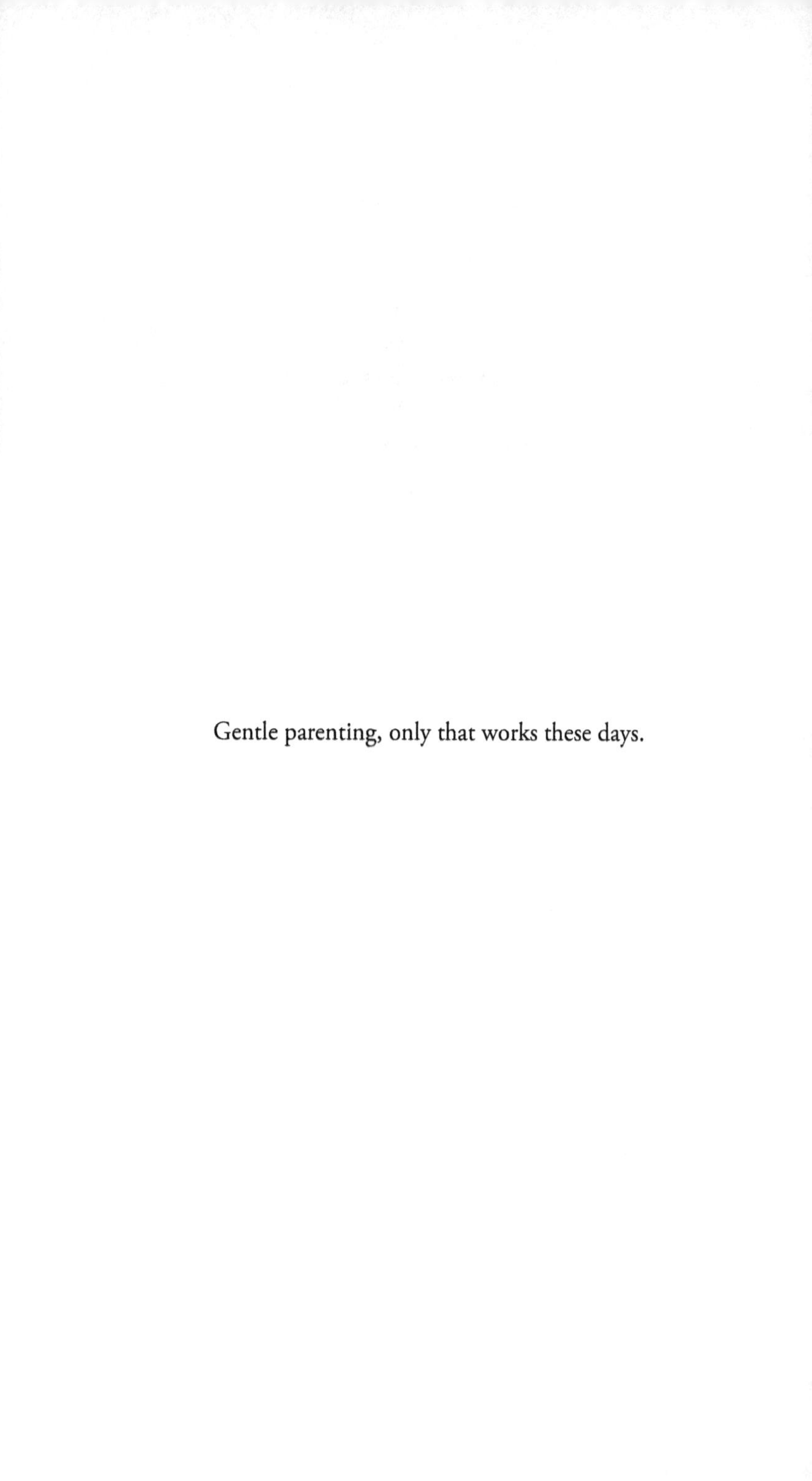

Gentle parenting, only that works these days.

Learn to read people

Initial days of people reading

Comes with a ton of over-confidence

Then comes a wave of self doubt

Because you see there is no set pattern

People, they come in different kinds

In random combinations.

But the gut instinct develops

As you feed in more and more data

Just like machine learning,

You learn to read people over-time

Just fine.

Impress not, who care not

We try impressing the public

When we are teenagers,

In your twenties,

That can exhaust your energy.

Energy, we direly need

For oh so many things.

Unless you are a stage performer

Do not waste your energy.

Impress not, who care not;

That includes your relatives.

Just do the basics.

Advising friends

My good friend of 14 years taught me,

(She always did the same)

The best advice comes

From friends

Who don't tell you what to do

Or throw random ideas at you

But help you make your decisions -

Yourself.

Who help you honestly see

How things look and seem to you,

And if you are seeing the same thing

Over and again

To really great friends,

Their image of you doesn't matter;

How you would look to the rest of the gang doesn't.

How you feel, surely does.

Do the same unto them.

Subtle comments, subtle warnings

People are more honest

And reveal their genuine intent

Not when they are being loud and dramatic

But when in passing they say something

Or give an indirect threat or warning.

Take it lightly at your own risk.

Fall out with friends

If you fall out with a new friend

It will most likely be gone,

Forgiven soon enough.

Or perhaps even forgotten soon

But a fallout with a childhood friend

That, that doesn't go away.

That scar, is here to stay.

You can't really mend that my friend

You will have to restart.

You aren't children anymore are you?

How then can you.... restart?

Observe anger, pain and failure

If it is your partner,

Observe how they deal with things

When angry,

When in pain

Or when they have failed.

That is who they really are.

The news

Don't believe everything

You see on TV.

Unless its the weather report ofcourse!

Was that precise all the time?

What really did happen then?

Talk to the locals.

Talk to auto drivers, taxi drivers, shopkeepers.

Do not believe everything you see

On the news.

Ignore red flags and die

Get a white board

If you constantly need to see things

To remember them.

White board it is then.

If you are okay with wasting paper,

Then sticky notes should be sufficient.

Listen to the well travelled

Don't deal with trauma-die permanently

When we don't accept

And filter out the good from the bad.

All from the same experience.

We may run away and reach

A trench even more so darker.

Because we thought to ourselves,

Anything unlike the trauma

Even with all the drama

Was better than that which

I ran oh so far way from.

Humour

You don't have to watch

Something funny

Or hear someone say

Things that tickle

You can find humour

In little everyday things

You CAN make yourself laugh

And the bonus is that

You will become wittier

And deal with people better.

Triggers

Until you find a way

To deal with them;

Until they can't hack

Your present moment anymore

Until they can't control you

Avoid them.

Then deal with them;

Spot their root (cause)

Deal with them

On a trial and error basis..

But if they affect how you function

Avoid them.

Productivity

Some people work in sequence;

Some do great in tandem;

Some only when inspired.

Find a pattern that fits you

The one who can precisely judge

If you have been productive

Or lacking

Is only you.

I work in tandem and when inspired, how about you?

Share traumatic experiences

What you share,

What you chose to bare

May be shameful to yourself

Or make the distant uncle

Call you shameless

But it might make someone

Indebted to you,

For your story

Made the difference,

Between life and death

For a stranger far and rare.

Choose Functionality

Invest more in skincare

And healthy skin habits

Than you do in outfits.

Invest in a good travel bag

In a functional tote

In reliable flats

And universal sneakers

In high waisted

Wide legged and perhaps cropped.

Choose functional and basic

That go with just about anything

A hobby

Not everything should be hustle,

Burnout can set you back by months if not years.

Keep a hobby, close to heart

Within arm's reach,

That can help you feel

Good about NOTHING

About the stillness and simplicity

Of everyday living.

And try keeeping touch with it

Once in 7 days perhaps?

It can even be home organisation.

Just quiet meditation with action.

Medical journal

Journal these,

As you would to productivity.

Track your health,

Symptoms,

Allergies and medications.

Its all about pattern my friend

And old school data keeping

That helps you make decisions

Better and smarter.

Especially if you are a mom

And you constantly forget things

Share it with baby.

Self-concept

Self love will not make you feel

More lonely and cut-off

Than you already are.

The right kind of self love

Must make you feel one with the whole

Must allow you to trust

Must allow you to be kinder

Must open your mind

But must protect you too,

It must energise the heart

To try new things.

How is that possible?

When you don't live as a shadow of your past

Or forcing yourself to;

When you realise

The true audience

Was really you.

Baby

To learn, unlearn and re-learn is undeniably a life long process. But to take sole credit for all the lessons shared here would be arrogant and misplaced.

Every single person I met on my journey so far, has taught me something probably even what my parents could not and that is a lesson I shall pass on to anyone listening and also to my dear Son. My child has been the invisible crutch holding me up in times of strife, has been and will always be the light in the room for many members of the family. I wish him all greatness, happiness and content in life and in someway hope this book will benefit him when he is old enough to read the things in here.

The lessons and sharing shall continue....